Sam Samuels
and his 7 sons

Written by John Lowndes

Illustrations by Brent Mottershead

MW00982002

AuthorHouse™
1663 Liberty Drive
Bloomington, IN 47403
www.authorhouse.com
Phone: 1 (800) 839-8640

© 2016 John Lowndes. All rights reserved.

No part of this book may be reproduced, stored in a retrieval system,
or transmitted by any means without the written permission of the author.

Published by AuthorHouse 10/19/2016

ISBN: 978-1-5246-4159-7 (sc)
ISBN: 978-1-5246-4160-3 (e)

Library of Congress Control Number: 2016915926

Print information available on the last page.

Any people depicted in stock imagery provided by Thinkstock are models,
and such images are being used for illustrative purposes only.
Certain stock imagery © Thinkstock.

This book is printed on acid-free paper.

Because of the dynamic nature of the Internet, any web addresses or links contained in this book may have changed
since publication and may no longer be valid. The views expressed in this work are solely those of the author and do not
necessarily reflect the views of the publisher, and the publisher hereby disclaims any responsibility for them.

authorHOUSE®

DEDICATION

I would like to dedicate this book to my family. Without them I would truly not be the man I am today! To Pam, who has never wavered in her love for me. To my boys who keep me thinking about new ideas for books, and to my parents who have always been there. Also to my many friends around the world from many diverse cultures and backgrounds who have taught me to love, learn, and live life fully! Finally I want to thank God who rescued me from certain destruction. I'm forever grateful.

John Lowndes

Hi, my name is Sam Samuels, and this is my farm!

I've lived here with my wife for most of my life,

But as I get old, I can't carry the hoe,

And I'm feeling some pain down deep in my toe!

The farm is so big,

We have horses and pigs.

There are even some cows,

And lots of big rigs.

The garden is great with carrots,

And grapes,

There's cantaloupes, pears,

And even some dates!

The barns are full, right up to the brim,

With some of the produce spilling over the rim.

The lawns need a cut, and I've not bathed my mutt,

And I'm just ready to sit on my butt!

So as you can see, there's too much for me!

And I've always dreamed of a trip to the sea.

So as I've got old, I'm being so bold,

I'm asking my sons to carry the load!

Son number one, 1 thought was like me,

But he liked to run, and just be free!

I asked him to come and help with the chores,

But the last I saw him, he was running through the doors.

"Please come help", I called after him.

"I can't right now, I'm off to the Gym,

Training for a race, and I'm gonna win!"

Son number 2 works in a Zoo,

He used to work on the farm cleaning the P....

He would help with the horses, the goats, and the ducks,

And was always around to help with the muck.

Until one day on a trip to a Zoo,

He saw an elephant, a lion and a leopard or two.

"Life on the farm has not been so bad,

But Dad I can see these animals need me real bad!"

Son number 3 seemed thrifty like me,

So I put him in charge of the shopping you see.

For here on the farm there are so many needs,

I've asked him to take care of them for me.

So off he would go and buy what we need,

Until one day he met this nice Swede.

Who offered him a job buying up feed.

I just hope he's not captured by greed.

Son number 4 would pour milk on the floor.

I would see him just gazing out the door.

His job on the farm was to care for the cows,

And now all the cats are singing happy Meows!

"Why did you pour milk on the floor son number 4?"

"I was lost in this book, and when I took a look,

It was like I was the one writing a book!"

So son number 4 went his own way,

And now he's a writer making great pay!

Son number 5, he liked to drive,

And on the tractors he would thrive!

I saw he had a gift, to drive very swift,

And now the soil gets a real lift!

He got going so fast, he was having a blast,

Now he's a racer and never comes in last!

In fact, he just won the nation's biggest race,

On our turbo charged tractor, he got first place!

Son number 6 was in charge of the seed,

He would plant the corn, the wheat, and always take the lead!

He would tell all the workers just what to do,

And make sure the crops were planted two by two!

Until one day he got offered a job,

He took over for a guy named Rob.

Now he doesn't lead here on the farm,

He has thousands who follow his great charm!

Son number 7 was always looking towards heaven,

He was our baker, and often forgot the leaven.

He would burn the toast, forget the roast,

and of his dinners we could not boast.

But I can't complain, he's walking another lane,

He's now easing other's pain!

Helping little orphans we saw was his gift,

Not just feeding us and giving us a lift.

At first I was sad, but then I began to see,

I don't need my sons to be just like me.

They each have a path, and it's my job to see,

How I can help find who they're called to be!

And that's not all I have to say,

I've learned some new lessons day by day,

That my children have dreams, and it's my job to be,

A Father who makes their journey as easy as can be!

Christmas is great, for we all make a date,

To meet on the farm, and no one's ever late,

For no matter what my children have become,

They each come home one by one!

Especially to see their Mom!

We have lots of laughs,

We look at funny pictures from the past!

We eat our farm food, and a turkey or two!

And, Momma makes Christmas pudding for the whole crew!

When my sons and their families head off for home,

Sometimes I feel really alone,

But I have found some hope,

And I'm learning not to mope!

So I let my sons go, and now don't you know,

I've found someone else shoveling the snow!

It's daughter number 8 who's been just great!

She's been working right beside me as my life gets late.

Daughters number 9, 10, 11, 12 have been just swell!

They've been helping on the farm and doing well.

But I'm not planning for all of their lives,

I'll wait and see what their motive drives!

So let this Father's tale of my life's trail,

Be a lesson to all, so we do not fail.

That our children have dreams,

And when life is not as it seems.

We need to let them go,

And encourage them to not be slow,

But to run this life's race,

And let them find their own place!

CPSIA information can be obtained
at www.ICGtesting.com
Printed in the USA
BVHW022127051118
532256BV00014B/48/P

9 781524 641597